Facts About Countries
France

Celia Tidmarsh

FRANKLIN WATTS
LONDON•SYDNEY

First published in 2005 by
Franklin Watts
96 Leonard Street, London
EC2A 4XD

Franklin Watts Australia
Level 17/207 Kent Street
Sydney NSW 2000

Facts About Countries is based on the Country
Files series published by Franklin Watts. It is
produced for Franklin Watts by Bender
Richardson White, PO Box 266, Uxbridge, UK.
Editors: Lionel Bender, Angela Royston
Designer and Page Make-up: Ben White
Picture Researcher: Cathy Stastny
Cover Make-up: Mike Pilley, Radius
Production: Kim Richardson

Graphics and Maps: Stefan Chabluk
Educational Advisor: Prue Goodwin, Institute of
Education, The University of Reading
Consultant: Dr Terry Jennings, a former
geography teacher and university lecturer. He is
now a full-time writer of children's geography
and science books.

A CIP catalogue record for this book is available
from the British Library.

ISBN 0-7496-6031-7
Dewey Classification 914.7

Printed in China

Picture Credits

Pages: 1: PhotoDisc Inc./Glen Allison. 3: Hutchison
Photo Library/Michael Macintyre. 4 top: PhotoDisc
Inc./Martial Colomb. 4 bottom: Hutchison Photo
Library/Robert Francis. 6: PhotoDisc Inc./Martial
Colomb. 8: DAS Photo/David Simson. 9: Eye
Ubiquitous/ Paul Thompson. 10-11 top: PhotoDisc
Inc./Martial Colomb. 10 bottom: Lionheart Books.
12: Hutchison Photo Library/J. C. Tordai.
13: Hutchison Photo Library. 15: Eye Ubiquitous/Julia
Waterlow. 17 top: DAS Photo/ David Simson.
18 bottom: Hutchison Photo Library/ J. G. Fuller.
18 top: DAS Photo/David Simson. 18 bottom: Lionheart
Books. 20: Hutchison Photo Library/Michael Macintyre.
22: PhotoDisc Inc./Sami Sarkis. 23: DAS Photo/David
Simson. 24: PhotoDisc Inc./ Sami Sarkis. 25: Eye
Ubiquitous/Mike Southern. 26: Adam Woolfit/Corbis
Images. 28: European Union Audiovisual Department.
29: Roger Rassmeyer/Corbis Images. 30: Lionheart
Books. 31: PhotoDisc Inc./Philippe Colon.
Cover photo: Owen Corben/Corbis Images Inc.

The Author

Celia Tidmarsh is a teacher-trainer specializing in Geography. She has written several books for children about different countries of the world.

Note to parents and teachers

Every effort has been made by the Publishers to ensure that the websites in this book are suitable for children, that they are of the highest educational value, and that they contain no inappropriate or offensive material. However, because of the nature of the Internet, it is impossible to guarantee that the contents of these sites will not be altered. We strongly advise that Internet access is supervised by a responsible adult.

Contents

Welcome to France

France is the largest country in Europe. France also controls the island of Corsica in the Mediterranean Sea.

France's borders

France is shaped like a hexagon — it has six sides. Three of these sides are on the coast. To the north is the English Channel and to the west is the Atlantic Ocean. The Mediterranean Sea lies to the south of France.

Mountains make up two sides of the country. The Pyrénées Mountains separate France from Spain. The Alps and Jura mountains separate France from Italy and Switzerland. Only the border with Belgium and Luxembourg is on flat land.

Above. **The village of Huez in the Alps is covered by snow in winter.**

Below. **A farm near Rouen in northern France.**

The Land

More than half of France is low, flat land but there are spectacular mountains in the south and east. The Massif Central is a range of extinct volcanoes.

Rivers

France has four main rivers — the Loire, the Seine, the Garonne and the Rhône. The longest river is the Loire. It flows from the Massif Central to the Atlantic Ocean. The River Seine flows through Paris, the capital city of France. The Garonne flows from the Pyrénées Mountains. The Rhône flows into the Mediterranean Sea.

Animals and Plants

Different areas of France are home to different types of animals and plants. For example:
- chamois deer live in the Alps
- wild boar live in forests in the north
- oak forests grow in the north and west
- olive trees grow in the south.

Below. **Burgundy in eastern France has a mild climate. It is good for growing grapes.**

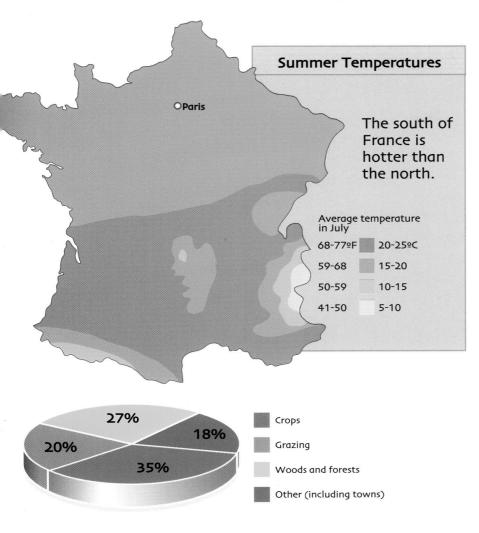

Summer Temperatures

The south of France is hotter than the north.

Average temperature in July

68-77°F	20-25°C
59-68	15-20
50-59	10-15
41-50	5-10

Crops — 18%
Grazing — 35%
Woods and forests — 20%
Other (including towns) — 27%

Above. **How the land is used.**

Above. **Average rainfall each month in Paris and Marseilles.**

Climate

Most of France has mild winters and warm summers. In the mountains, the winters are much colder and it often snows heavily there. Near the Mediterranean Sea, it is hot and dry in summer and warm in winter. The Mistral is a cold wind that blows down the Rhône valley at certain times of the year.

Web Search ▶▶

▶ www.abritel.fr/uk/meteo 24.php
Weather forecast for France.

▶ www.meteofrance.com/FR/ index.jsp
Weather and climate for France.

▶ www.franceguide.com
Maps, travel and tourist information about France.

The People

Nearly 59 million people live in France. Many French families have only one or two children. For many years, the number of children has been falling and the number of old people rising.

A mixture of peoples

The French are descended from several peoples. The Celtic Gauls moved into the area between 1500 and 500 BCE. The Romans came in 52 BCE. Then, in about CE 500, the Franks arrived from west Germany. Recently, people have come to live in France from the Middle East, North Africa, South-east Asia, Russia and Portugal.

Above. **The huge Galeries Lafayette department store in Paris sells all kinds of goods.**

Below. **How the ages of the French population have changed since 1970.**

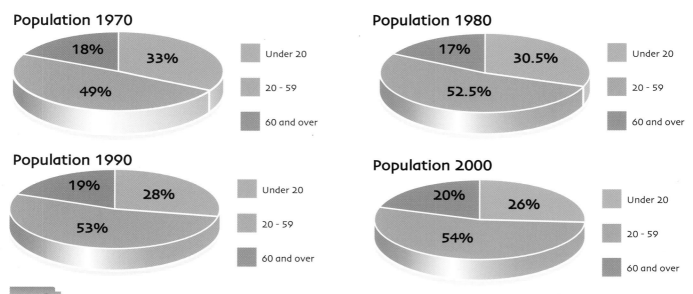

Population 1970

- 18%
- 33%
- 49%
- Under 20
- 20 - 59
- 60 and over

Population 1980

- 17%
- 30.5%
- 52.5%
- Under 20
- 20 - 59
- 60 and over

Population 1990

- 19%
- 28%
- 53%
- Under 20
- 20 - 59
- 60 and over

Population 2000

- 20%
- 26%
- 54%
- Under 20
- 20 - 59
- 60 and over

A common language

French is the official language of France. Some areas of France have kept their traditional languages, too. Flemish is spoken in the far north, Breton in Brittany, Basque and Catalan in the Pyrénées, and Provençal in Provence. French is also the official language in Switzerland, Belgium and parts of Canada and Africa.

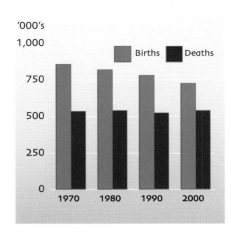

Above. Changes in the numbers of births and deaths in France since 1970.

Left. Artists from all over the world sit and paint in Montmartre in Paris. In the background is the Sacre-Coeur, one of the city's oldest churches.

Web Search ▶▶

▶ www.paris.org
Information about Paris.

▶ www.info-france-usa.org/
kids/
All about France for children.

▶ www.brittany-bretagne.com
Guide to Brittany, the north-west of France.

▶ www.odci.gov/cia/
publications/factbook/geos/
fr.html
Facts, figures and maps of France.

9

Town and Country Life

More French people live in towns and cities than in the countryside. During the last 50 years, many people have moved to the cities to find work.

More crowded areas

The largest cities include Paris, Marseilles and Lyons. People live in the city centres and suburbs. Many people farm on the flat land around the cities and near the coasts. Fewer people live in the mountain areas.

Below. Many French villages lie in wooded areas surrounded by farmland.

People on the move

French people have moved to cities to work in offices, shops, factories and banks. Since the 1970s, many people from other countries have also gone to French cities to work and study. Some French people have moved to the south of France because the climate there is more pleasant.

Homes

In cities, many people live in modern, high-rise apartment buildings. Others live in houses in the suburbs. In the countryside, empty farmhouses may be rented to tourists.

Above. **The Eiffel Tower, a famous landmark in the centre of Paris.**

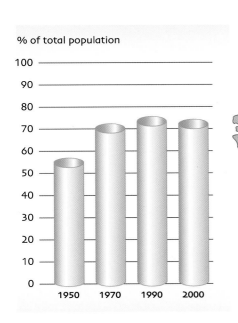

% of total population

Above. **The increase in the percentage of people who live in cities and towns.**

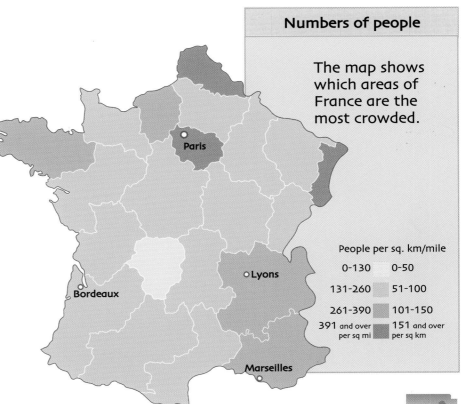

Numbers of people

The map shows which areas of France are the most crowded.

Paris

Lyons

Bordeaux

Marseilles

People per sq. km/mile

0-130	0-50
131-260	51-100
261-390	101-150
391 and over per sq mi	151 and over per sq km

Above. **This fisherman has been catching crabs.**

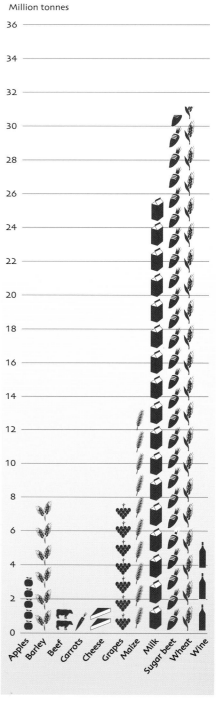

Million tonnes

Apples, Barley, Beef, Carrots, Cheese, Grapes, Maize, Milk, Sugar beet, Wheat, Wine

Above. **Farm products each year, by weight.**

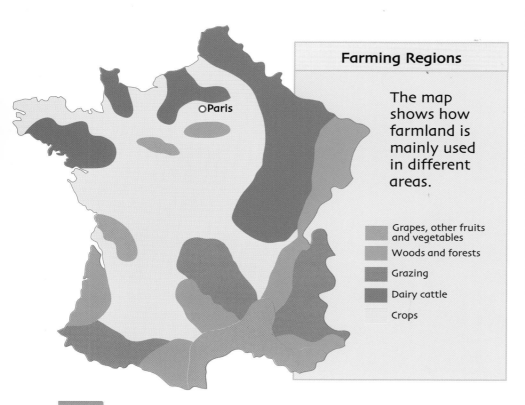

o Paris

Farming Regions

The map shows how farmland is mainly used in different areas.

Grapes, other fruits and vegetables

Woods and forests

Grazing

Dairy cattle

Crops

Farming and Fishing

Fishing

Fishing is an important way of making money along the coasts of France.

Small fishing boats fish from most seaside villages. Larger boats fish off the coasts of Iceland, Canada, west Africa and Europe.

French people eat about 30 kilograms of fish a year per person. People in the UK eat only 20 kilograms.

Only a few people work in farming and fishing. Yet they provide most of the food French people eat. They also sell food to other countries.

Farming

More than half the land in France is used for farming. Wheat and corn are grown on low-lying land. Grapes, peaches, lemons and other fruit are grown in the south of France. Sheep are kept in the mountains. Cattle are kept for milk or for beef in most areas except around the Mediterranean. It is too hot there for cattle.

Exporting food

Except for the United States, France exports more food than any other country. French farmers use machines, fertilizers and pesticides to help them grow large amounts of crops and to raise large numbers of animals.

Left. **Farmers pick grapes in a vineyard near Cahors, south-west France.**

13

Resources and Industry

Most people work in service industries such as tourism, insurance and banking. France uses its rich supplies of minerals in power stations and factories.

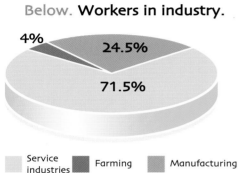

Below. **Workers in industry.**

4%
24.5%
71.5%

Service industries   Farming   Manufacturing

Service industries

More and more French people are working in jobs that offer a service to other people. For example, they work for hotels, shops, banks, airlines, and television and computer companies. France is also a world leader in medicine and healthcare.

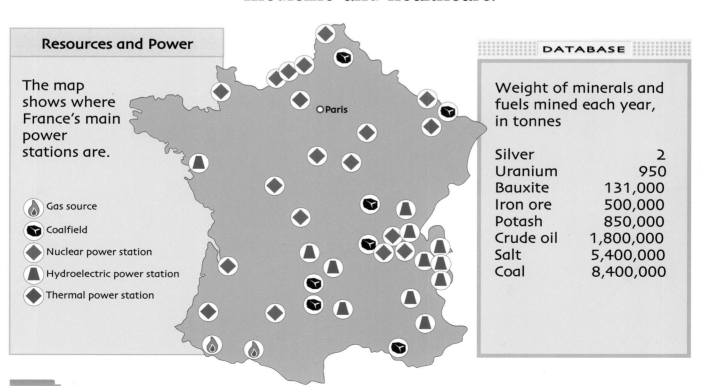

Resources and Power

The map shows where France's main power stations are.

🜂 Gas source

⬢ Coalfield

◆ Nuclear power station

▲ Hydroelectric power station

◆ Thermal power station

○ Paris

DATABASE

Weight of minerals and fuels mined each year, in tonnes

Silver	2
Uranium	950
Bauxite	131,000
Iron ore	500,000
Potash	850,000
Crude oil	1,800,000
Salt	5,400,000
Coal	8,400,000

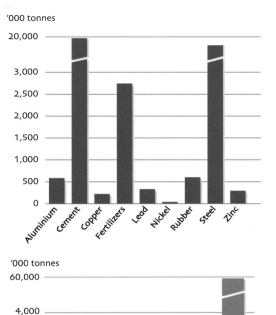

'000 tonnes

Aluminium / Cement / Copper / Fertilizers / Lead / Nickel / Rubber / Steel / Zinc

'000 tonnes

Cars / Commercial vehicles / Radios / TVs / Tyres

Left. **Weight of goods produced by French factories each year.**

Above. **A tanker docks at an oil refinery at Le Havre in northern France.**

Mining and manufacturing

Mines in north-west France produce salt, bauxite and other minerals. Iron and steel are used to build ships, trains and cars. Citroën and Renault are two well-known car makers. Aeroplanes and spacecraft are also made in France.

Power stations

Power stations generate electricity. More than 80 per cent of France's electricity is generated by nuclear power stations.

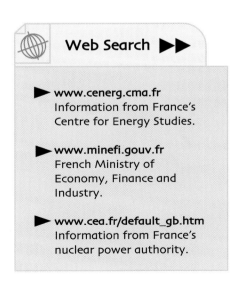

Web Search ►►

► www.cenerg.cma.fr
Information from France's Centre for Energy Studies.

► www.minefi.gouv.fr
French Ministry of Economy, Finance and Industry.

► www.cea.fr/default_gb.htm
Information from France's nuclear power authority.

Transport

Travel in Paris

THE METRO: this is Paris's underground railway. There are so many stations that nowhere is further than 500 metres from a métro station.

BUSES: there are plenty of bus routes and special bus lanes on main roads, but heavy traffic often slows down the buses.

TAXIS: these can be hired in the street or from special taxi ranks.

France has excellent road, railway and airline links between its cities and other countries. These links are also used to transport goods.

Roads and railways

It is easy to travel quickly from one end of France to the other. Cars, buses and lorries drive along motorways, called autoroutes. Travelling by high-speed train (called TGVs) is even faster. Many people travel between cities by aeroplane because France is so big.

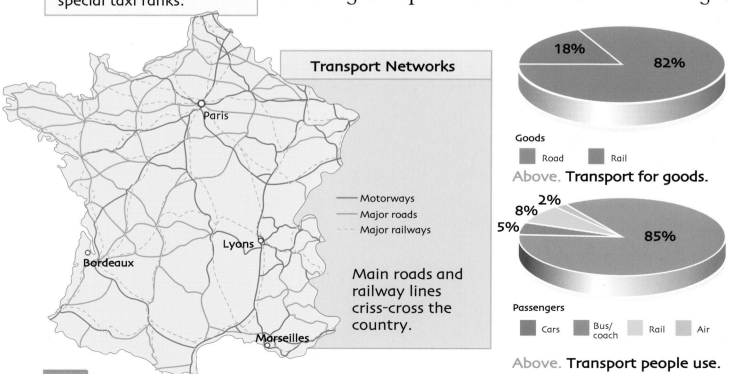

Transport Networks

— Motorways
— Major roads
--- Major railways

Main roads and railway lines criss-cross the country.

18%   82%

Goods
■ Road   ■ Rail

Above. **Transport for goods.**

2%
8%
5%   85%

Passengers
■ Cars   ■ Bus/coach   ■ Rail   ■ Air

Above. **Transport people use.**

Above. Eurostar trains take passengers from Paris to London through the Channel Tunnel.

Left. Passengers leave the Métro, Paris's underground railway.

Web Search ►►

► www.smartweb.fr/aero/index.html
Paris's airports and flights.

► www.sncf.com/indexe.htm
French railways.

► www.aboutfrance.bravepages.com/travel.htm
Travel to and in France.

Travelling to other countries

Ferries sail from France to Spain, England, Ireland and North Africa. Most French cities have international airports. Roads and railways are linked to the rest of Europe.

Above. **Children in French schools use computers more and more. Every school follows the same currriculum.**

Right. **Many villages have a small local school. Here, children of different ages share one teacher in the same classroom.**

Education

French children go to school from the age of six to 16. Most children go to public schools, which are free. Some children go to fee-paying, private schools.

French schools

Some children go to nursery when they are two years old. All children go to primary school from age six to 11. Then children go to secondary school. When they are 15 or 16 years old, they decide whether to stay at school or to train for a job. Those who stay at school can choose to study economics, languages or science, and other subjects. When they are 18, students take an exam known as the general baccalauréat. They must pass this exam to study at a university.

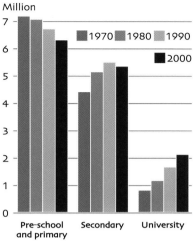

Above. **Changes in the numbers of students in schools and universities.**

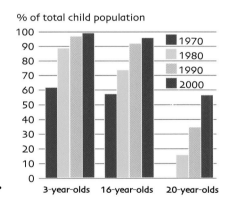

Above. **Percentages of children in education.**

The school day

Most children go to school on Saturday mornings as well as from 8.30 a.m. to 4.30 p.m. Monday to Friday. Wednesday afternoons are used for sport instead of lessons. In all schools, children do not have to wear a school uniform. The summer holiday lasts nine weeks, which is longer than in most other European countries.

Web Search ▶▶

▶ www.education.fr
The French education system.

▶ www.frenchentree.com/ fe-education/
Going to school in France.

Sport and Leisure

French people enjoy their leisure time. They watch and play many sports. Most families have at least one holiday a year.

Sport

French people like to watch and play tennis, football, basketball and rugby. They also like cycling. In summer, they swim in lakes and the sea, and hike in the mountains. In winter, they go skiing and snowboarding.

Right. Tour de France cyclists race in teams. The cyclists are followed by race supervisors, police and TV camera crews.

Holidays and tourism

French people take long holidays in the summer. Many families go to the seaside. Others rent gîtes (holiday homes) in the countryside or travel around Europe.

Every year, about 60 million tourists visit France from other countries. Many of them visit the EuroDisney theme park near Paris. Others visit tourist sites in Paris, Bayeux and Chartres or go to beaches in the south. The amount of money spent by tourists in France has greatly increased since 1980.

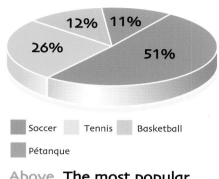

Soccer · Tennis · Basketball · Pétanque

Above. **The most popular sports played. Pétanque is a type of bowls played with metal balls.**

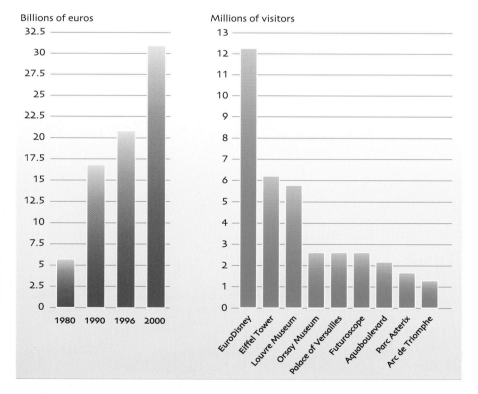

Above. **Amount of money spent by tourists in France.**

Above. **The most popular tourist sites in France.**

🌐 **Web Search** ▶▶

▶ www.tifonet.it/soccer/
France win 1998 World Cup football tournament.

▶ www.cyclingnews.com/
Tour de France cycle race and other cycling news and information.

▶ www.tourisme.fr
French Tourist Office.

▶ www.paris.org
Tourist information about Paris.

Daily Life and Religion

French people spend their days working, shopping and enjoying themselves. Eating at restaurants is an important part of French life.

Shops

French people buy much of their food from small shops in their village or town. These shops often specialize in certain foods. For example, charcuteries sell cooked meats and boulangeries sell bread. People also shop at hypermarchés, which are giant supermarkets built on the outskirts of towns.

% of households owning

Above. **Electronic goods that French people own.**

Working hours

The working day starts at about 8 a.m. and ends at 6 p.m., often with a 2-hour lunch break. At weekends, many shops are open, but offices, building sites and factories are closed.

Right. **Notre Dame in Paris is one of the most famous churches in France.**

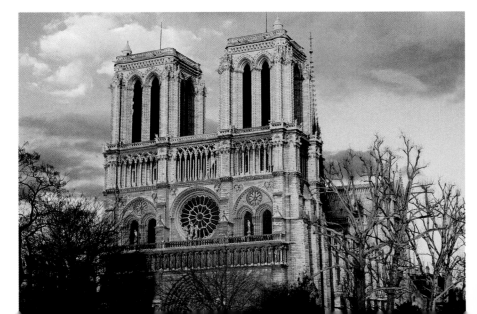

Left. **Food for sale at a street market in France.**

Web Search ▶▶

▶ www.sante.gouv.fr
General health information.

▶ www.defense.gouv.fr
The Ministry of Defence.

▶ www.info-europe.fr
Information about everyday life in France.

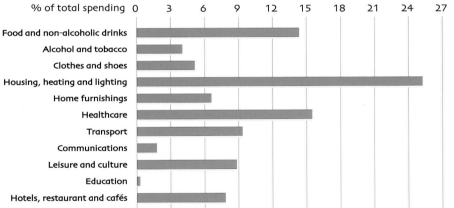

% of total spending	0	3	6	9	12	15	18	21	24	27
Food and non-alcoholic drinks										
Alcohol and tobacco										
Clothes and shoes										
Housing, heating and lighting										
Home furnishings										
Healthcare										
Transport										
Communications										
Leisure and culture										
Education										
Hotels, restaurant and cafés										

Left. **How French households spend their money.**

Religion

There is no official state religion in France. Most people say they are Roman Catholic although few of them go to church regularly. More than 3 million people in France are Muslim. There are also about 1 million Protestants and 500,000 Jews.

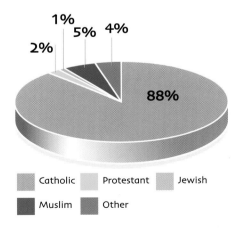

1%   5%   4%
2%
88%

Catholic   Protestant   Jewish
Muslim   Other

Above. **Percentages of people of different religions.**

Arts and Media

France has world-famous painters, writers and musicians. Some lived hundreds of years ago, but others are still alive today.

Museums, galleries and cinemas

Paris has many well-known museums and art galleries. In Paris you can see the work of Monet, Renoir and other painters. The world's first cinema opened in Paris in 1895. Today, more people in France go to the cinema than in other European countries. Futuroscope, near Poitiers, is a theme park about cinema. It opened in 1987.

Below. **Palais Longchamp in Marseilles. France has many palaces and fine houses.**

Left. These unusual fountains are outside the Pompidou Centre in Paris.

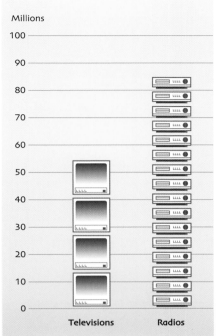

Millions

Televisions   Radios

Above. Number of TVs and radios owned in France.

Newspapers

About 40 cities in France publish their own newspapers every day. Some, such as *Le Monde* and *Le Figaro*, are sold all over France and in other countries, too.

Television and radio

France has 116 different television channels, including cable and pay-TV. There are also hundreds of radio stations. They are mostly local stations that broadcast only in French.

Web Search ▶▶

▶ www.lemonde.fr/
The French newspaper *Le Monde*.

▶ www.cplus.fr/
Canal+ TV broadcast station.

▶ www.paris.org/Musees/
Museums in Paris.

▶ www.futuroscope.fr/
Futuroscope theme park.

▶ www.louvre.fr/
Louvre museum in Paris.

Above. **The government office building in the town of Nancy in north-east France.**

Below. **French territories and départements abroad.**

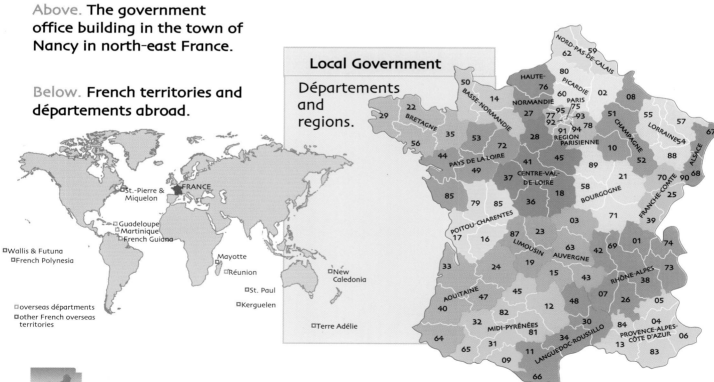

St.-Pierre & Miquelon
FRANCE
Guadeloupe
Martinique
French Guiana
Wallis & Futuna
French Polynesia
Mayotte
Réunion
New Caledonia
St. Paul
Kerguelen
overseas départements
other French overseas territories
Terre Adélie

Local Government

Départements and regions.

NORD-PAS-DE-CALAIS
59
62
50
HAUTE-
80
BASSE-NORMANDIE
14
76
PICARDIE
02
08
29
22
BRETAGNE
NORMANDIE
60
PARIS
51
55
57
27
77 95 93
LORRAINE 54
67
35
53
72
28
92
78
ALSACE
56
91 94
10
52
88
68
44
PAYS DE LA LOIRE
41
45
REGION PARISIENNE
89
21
70
90
49
CENTRE-VAL-
DE-LOIRE
58
FRANCHE-COMTE
25
85
79
85
37
18
BOURGOGNE
39
36
03
71
POITOU-CHARENTES
87
23
17
16
LIMOUSIN
63
69
01
74
33
24
19
AUVERGNE
42
RHONE-ALPES
73
15
43
38
AQUITAINE
47
45
48
07
26
05
40
82
12
30
84
PROVENCE-ALPES-
CÔTE D'AZUR
06
32
MIDI-PYRÉNÉES
81
34
LANGUEDOC-ROUSSILLO
13
83
64
65
31
11
09
66

26

Government

France is a democracy ruled by a parliament. Parliament is made up of the National Assembly and the Senate.

Elections

The president is the head of state. He or she is elected every seven years. The National Assembly has 577 deputies who are elected by the French people every five years. The Senate has 321 senators who are elected by the National Assembly and local officials every nine years.

Regions and départements

France is divided into 22 regions. Each region is divided into areas called départements. Each département is governed by a local council. The members of the council are elected by local people.

Overseas départements

Five of France's départements are abroad. They are mainly islands that are ruled by France. They have the same laws, school system and currency as France.

Départements

Every département has a name and a number. Some are named after local rivers.

The number of the département is used on car registration plates. Number 75 is for the centre of Paris.

Web Search

▶ www.french-at-a-touch.com/Countries/france.htm
Information on the regions and départements.

▶ www.premier-ministre.gouv.fr/en/
France's prime minister.

▶ www.assemblee-nat.fr/
The National Assembly.

▶ www.tahiti.com/
The island of Tahiti in French Polynesia.

27

Historical Events

1500–500 BCE The Gauls move into France

52 BCE–CE 500 France is overrun by the Romans

768–814 Charlemagne, king of the Franks, rules much of France

1337–1453 War between France and England

1562–98 Wars of religion between Catholics and Protestants

1789 French Revolution begins

1792 France is made a republic

1799–1804 Napoleon Bonaparte becomes Emperor of France

1804–12 French army occupies much of Europe

1815 Napoleon defeated at Battle of Waterloo

1870–71 France defeated by Prussians

1914–18 World War I

1939–45 World War II

Place in the World

France has played an important part in European history for more than 1,500 years. It is a key member of the United Nations and other world organizations.

European Union

Perhaps France's greatest achievement is the setting up of the European Union (EU) after World War II. The idea of the EU is to unite European countries. The EU helps the countries who belong to it to become wealthier. Most of France's trade is with other members of the EU. France also keeps strong links with its old colonies in Africa and Asia.

Below. **A historic meeting held in Paris on 9 May 1950. Leaders from France, Germany, Italy, Belgium, Luxembourg and the Netherlands help set up today's European Union.**

Left. France's rocket site at Kourou in French Guiana. This rocket took satellites for European television companies into space.

Web Search ▶▶

▶ www.franceway.com/
French history.

▶ www.ambafrance-au.org/
Information about France
from a French Embassy.

▶ www.diplomatie.gouv.fr/
French Ministry of Foreign
Affairs.

▶ www.legifrance.gouv.fr/
French government and
parliament.

▶ www.euro.gouv.fr/
French Ministry of Finance.

▶ www.europa.eu.int/
index_en.htm
Information about the EU.

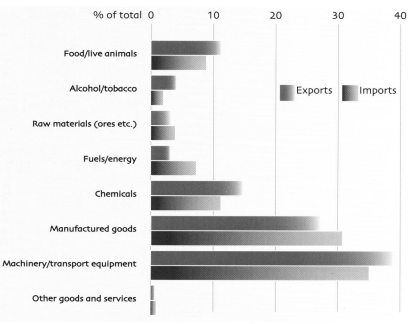

% of total

| | 0 | 10 | 20 | 30 | 40 |

Food/live animals
Alcohol/tobacco
Raw materials (ores etc.)
Fuels/energy
Chemicals
Manufactured goods
Machinery/transport equipment
Other goods and services

Exports Imports

Left. France's main imports and exports.

Area:
547,026 sq km

Population:
58,519,000

Capital city:
Paris (pop. 2,152,423)

Other major cities:
Marseilles, Lyons, Toulouse

Longest river:
Loire (1,012 km)

Highest mountain:
Mont Blanc (4,807m)

Largest lake:
Lac Léman (239sq km)

Flag:
Blue, white and red vertical stripes. Dates from the French Revolution in 1789. Blue and red were the city colours of Paris where the revolution began. White was the old royal colour.

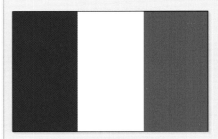

Official language:
French

Currency:
euro

Major resources:
Uranium, potash, salt, oil, iron ore

Major exports:
Machinery/transport (cars, tyres, aircraft); manufactured goods (TVs, radios, computers)

National holidays:
1 January: New Year's Day
Late March/early April: Easter

1 May: May Day
8 May: Victory Day, WWII
Mid-May/mid-June: Whit Monday
14 July: Bastille Day
15 August: Assumption Day
1 November: All Saints' Day
11 November: Remembrance Day
25 December: Christmas

Religions:
Roman Catholic, Muslim, Protestant, Jewish

Key Words

BAUXITE
A mineral containing lots of aluminium.

BORDER
Line that marks the edge of a country.

CLIMATE
The usual weather at different times of the year.

COLONY
A country ruled or governed by another country.

CURRICULUM
Programme of study in schools.

DEMOCRACY
System in which people elect the government.

DESCENDED
Related through people who lived a long time ago.

ECONOMICS
The study of business, industry and finance.

ELECTED
Officials voted for by the people of the country.

EURO
The currency used by most European Union countries.

EUROPEAN UNION (EU)
A group of more than 20 European countries that trade with each other on equal terms.

EXPORTS
Goods sold to other countries.

EXTINCT
No longer active.

IMPORTS
Goods bought from other countries.

MINERALS
The raw materials of rocks. They include coal, sand, iron and other metals.

NUCLEAR POWER
Electricity made by splitting atoms of uranium.

OFFICIAL LANGUAGE
Language usually used by people working in schools, government and law courts.

PESTICIDES
Chemicals used to kill pests that attack plants.

POPULATION
The number of people in a particular area.

POTASH
A salt used in fertilizers.

REPUBLIC
Country in which the head of state is elected or appointed. A republic does not have a king or queen who inherits the title.

RESOURCES
Supplies of natural materials such as coal and iron ore.

SERVICE INDUSTRIES
Industries that provide a service to people rather than make products.

SPECIALIZE
Concentrate on only one particular area or product.

SUBURBS
Areas of housing around the centre of towns and cities.

TGV (Train de Grande Vitesse)
A type of train that travels at speeds of up to 300kph between cities.

TRADE
Buying and selling goods.

Index